Social Media Success for Small Businesses: The Young Entrepreneur's Approach For Sustainable Growth And Profitability in the online space

Jamal Kreiger

All rights reserved. No part of this publication may be reproduced, distributed, or transmitted in any form or by any means, including photocopying, recording, or other electronic or mechanical methods, without prior written permission of the publisher, except in the case of brief quotations embodied in critical reviews and certain other non-commercial uses permitted by copyright law.

Copyright @ Jamal Kreiger, 2024

Table of Contents

CHAPTER I	6
CHAPTER II	12
CHAPTER III	15
CHAPTER IV	19
CHAPTER V	28
CHAPTER VI	37
CHAPTER VII	50
CHAPTER VIII	61
CHAPTER IX	64
CHAPTER X	72
CHAPTER XI	77
CHAPTER XII	80
CHAPTER XIII	88
CHAPTER XIV	93
CONCLUSION	97

DESCRIPTION
Social Media Success for Small Businesses: The Young Entrepreneur's Approach For Sustainable Growth And Profitability in the online space

Social media has emerged as the key component of effective marketing plans in the current digital environment, catering to companies of all kinds. However, small firms may find it difficult to navigate this constantly changing landscape. In this situation, "Social Media Success for Small Businesses" can be your go-to resource for learning social media marketing techniques and growing your small business to new height
Experienced marketing professional [Jamal Kreiger] demystifies the world of social media in this extensive handbook, breaking down intricate methods into manageable stages designed especially for small business owners. This book covers everything, from creating intriguing content to interacting with your audience and making the most out of your advertising money.

Learn how to use social media sites like Facebook, Instagram, Twitter, and LinkedIn to promote your brand, improve website traffic, and eventually increase sales. Discover the techniques for writing content that people want to share, developing a devoted fan base, and turning followers into devoted clients. However, "Social Media Success For Small Businesses" is more about strategy than techniques. You'll delve into the psychology of social media users to learn what motivates them and how to craft material that will appeal to them. Discover how to use influencer relationships, user-generated content, and storytelling to strengthen the message of your business and build real connections with your target audience.

"Social Media Success For Small Businesses" gives you the skills and information you need to succeed in the cutthroat world of social media marketing with its useful advice, real-world examples, and simple-to-follow action plans. This book will enable you to take charge of your online presence and turn your small business into a social media powerhouse, regardless of experience level as an entrepreneur.

Prepare to enhance your company with "Social Media Success For Small Businesses" and realize the full potential of social media marketing so that your rivals can't take the limelight away from you.

CHAPTER I
INTRODUCTION

Social media has completely changed how companies of all sizes communicate with their clientele. Social media, in particular, offers small businesses an affordable and effective platform to expand their brand and connect with more customers. However, small business owners may find it difficult to know where to begin and how to get the most out of their social media efforts due to the abundance of social media platforms and tactics available.

This comprehensive handbook fills that need. Small business owners will gain a thorough understanding of social media marketing from it, along with tips for using different social media platforms and best practices. Everything a small business owner needs to know to thrive in the always-changing field of social media marketing will be covered in this guide, from setting up a social media presence to interacting with clients and tracking results.

This guide will provide you with the skills and information you need to successfully market your small business on social media and eventually spur growth and success, regardless of whether you are just getting started or want to improve your current presence. So let's get started and realize the full potential of social media for your business by exploring our comprehensive guide to social media marketing for small businesses.

A. Social Media Marketing Definition.
The practice of promoting a good or service using social media platforms and websites is known as social media marketing. This can involve producing and disseminating content, interacting with influencers and followers, and managing sponsored social media campaigns. In the end, social media marketing aims to create leads and sales by raising brand awareness and increasing website traffic. It is an essential part of digital marketing, and it is always changing as new social media features and platforms appear.

B. The Value of Social Media Advertising to Small Businesses
In this digital age, social media marketing has become a vital tool for small enterprises. Businesses now have access to a large audience

of potential clients thanks to the growth of social media platforms like Facebook, Instagram, Twitter, and LinkedIn.

The following are some main arguments in favor of social media marketing for small businesses:

1. Enhanced Recognition of the Brand

Social media platforms are a great way for small businesses to expand their reach and visibility because they have billions of active users. Small businesses can boost their online presence by consistently creating brand awareness and getting their name out to potential customers.

2. Economy-Friendly Promotion

A fraction of the price of traditional advertising strategies is spent on a variety of advertising possibilities provided by social media sites. Ads are a cost-effective approach for small businesses to market their goods and services since they can reach a highly targeted audience and monitor their success.

3. Enhanced Interaction with Customers

Social media makes it possible for companies and their clients to communicate directly. Social networking is a useful tool for small businesses to reply to questions from clients, handle issues, and get feedback. In addition to fostering a sense of community, this grows a foundation of devoted clients.

4. Focused Advertising

Businesses can target specific demographics, interests, and behaviors through social media platforms' sophisticated targeting features. By doing this, small businesses can increase the likelihood of conversion by ensuring that their marketing efforts are directed towards the appropriate target.

5. Enhanced SEO and Website Traffic

Social media can increase website traffic for small businesses by advertising new offerings, blog posts, and deals. Considering that social media signals are now taken into account by SEO algorithms, this can help raise a business's search engine rating.

6. Analysis of Competitors

Social media can be used by small firms to monitor and assess the tactics of their rivals. Businesses can learn valuable lessons from their competitors' social media presence and modify their own marketing strategy accordingly.

7. Obtaining Useful Analytics and Insights

Social media platforms provide statistics and

insights that can give useful details on the demographics, interests, and behaviors of a small business's audience. Businesses can use this information to better focus their content to appeal to their target audience and make educated marketing decisions.

8. Influencer Marketing Opportunity

Influencer marketing—in which companies collaborate with well-known social media users to promote their goods or services—benefits greatly from the use of social media. By doing this, small enterprises can expand their consumer base and win over new clients' credibility and confidence.

9. User-Friendly

The majority of social media sites are simple to use and manage, making them accessible to small businesses with little funding or background in marketing. Additionally, they provide a range of tools and resources to assist companies in successfully developing and maintaining their social media presence.

10. Measurable Outcomes

For small businesses, one of the biggest advantages of social media marketing is the opportunity to monitor and assess the success of their campaigns. This enables companies to monitor the effects of their social media marketing directly and tweak their plans for better results.

CHAPTER II

FUNDAMENTALS OF SOCIAL MEDIA FOR SOCIAL MEDIA MARKETING

Fundamentals of social media encompass various key principles and strategies essential for effectively utilizing social platforms for personal or business purposes. Some fundamental aspects include:

1. **Know your target audience: Start by targeting a specific audience** segment with your social media campaigns and content. Monitor the performance of your campaigns, track key metrics, and gather feedback to assess how well you are reaching and engaging with your target audience. Use this data to refine your targeting strategies and adjust your approach as needed. Divide your target audience into distinct segments based on demographics, psychographics, behaviors, interests, or other criteria. This segmentation will help you tailor your messaging, content, and marketing strategies to address the specific needs and preferences of each segment.

Knowing your target audience's demographics,

interests, and behaviors is crucial for creating relevant and engaging content.

2.**Content Strategy:** Developing a content strategy involves planning and creating content that resonates with your audience, aligns with your brand identity, and serves your objectives.

3. **Engagement:** Actively engaging with your audience by responding to comments, messages, and mentions fosters a sense of community and builds trust.

4. **Consistency:** Consistently posting valuable content and maintaining a regular presence on social media helps keep your audience engaged and strengthens your brand presence.

5. **Platform Selection**: Choosing the right social media platforms based on your target audience, business goals, and type of content is essential for maximizing your reach and impact.

6. **Analytics and Measurement:** Tracking metrics such as engagement, reach, and conversions allows you to evaluate the effectiveness of your social media efforts and make data-driven decisions.

7. Adaptability: Social media platforms and trends are constantly evolving, so staying updated with changes and adapting your strategy accordingly is essential for long-term success.

8. Authenticity: Authenticity and transparency are valued by social media users. Being genuine in your interactions and sharing authentic stories helps build stronger connections with your audience.

By mastering these fundamentals, individuals and businesses can leverage the power of social media to build brand awareness, engage with their audience, drive traffic, and achieve their goals effectively.

CHAPTER III

UNDERSTANDING YOUR TARGET AUDIENCE

Understanding your target audience is a pivotal aspect of social media marketing for small businesses. By relating and connecting with the right audience, businesses can produce further targeted and effective marketing campaigns that reverberate with implicit customers. Then are some crucial points to consider when understanding your target audience in relation to social media marketing

1. **Demographics:** Start by defining the demographic characteristics of your target audience, including age, gender, position, income position, education, and occupation. This information will help you conform your social media content and advertisements to appeal to your target demographic

2. **Psychographics**: In addition to demographic data, consider the psychographic traits of your audience, similar as interests, pursuits, values, life choices, and stations. Understanding these aspects can help you produce content that aligns

with your audience's preferences and provocations.

3. **Behavior**: analyse your audiences online behaviour,
including the social media platforms they use, the type of content they engage with, the frequency of their online engagements, and their purchasing patterns. By understanding how your audience behaves online, you can conform your social media strategy to effectively reach and engage with them.

4. **Pain Points and Needs:** Identify the pain points, challenges, and requirements of your target audience. By addressing these issues in your social media content, you can place your business as a precious result provider and make trust with your audience.

5. **Communication Preferences**: Determine how your target audience prefers to communicate and engage with brands on social media. Some cult may prefer visual content like vids and images, while others may prefer written content or interactive pates. Conform your

content formats and messaging to meet the communication preferences of your audience.

6. Conduct Analysis: Conduct a competitive analysis to understand how your challengers are engaging with their target audience on social media. Identify gaps and openings where you can separate your brand and offer unique value to your audience.

7. Feedback and Data Analysis: Gather feedback from your living guests and dissect social media criteria to gain perceptivity into your audience's preferences, interests, and actions. Use this data to upgrade your social media strategy and continually ameliorate your targeting sweats.

By understanding the above, small businesses can produce more individualized and effective marketing campaigns that drive engagement, increase brand mindfulness, and eventually, induce leads and deals. Taking the time to dissect and connect with your audience on social media will help you make lasting connections and grow your business successfully.

Identifying Your Target Audience

Identifying your target audience is crucial in developing a successful social media marketing strategy for your small business.

There are some tips and strategies to help you effectively identify your target audience, of which if followed meticulously, you will effectively identify your target audience for social media marketing and knitter your efforts to reach and engage with the right clients for your small business. An important point to note is that audience identification is an ongoing process, and it's essential to continuously dissect data, test, and upgrade your targeting to maximise the impact of your social media marketing efforts.

CHAPTER IV

HOW TO CHOOSE TARGET AUDIENCE FOR SOCIAL MEDIA MARKETING

Choosing the right target audience for your social media marketing efforts is essential for reaching the right people with your messaging and maximizing the effectiveness of your juggernauts.

Tips To Consider When Choosing Target Audience
To outline these tips, these are some questions to guide you

1. **What business/ product are you selling?** Start by having a clear understanding of your business, products, and services. Identify your unique selling points, value proposition, and the benefits you offer to guests. This understanding will help you determine who would be interested in what you have to offer.

2. **What are your social media marketing objectives?** Determine your social media marketing goals and objectives. Are you looking to increase brand mindfulness,

drive website business, induce leads, boost deals, or enhance client engagement? Your objectives will impact the type of audience you target and the messaging you use.

3. **Who are your existing customers:** Look at your current client base and dissect their demographics, psychographics, actions, and preferences. Identify common characteristics, interests, requirements, and pain points among your existing clients to guide your target audience selection.

4. **Who are your competitors?** Research your industry, competitors, and target request to gain perceptivity into client trends, preferences, and actions. Identify market segments, trends, and openings that align with your business objects and immolations.

5. **Who are your target audience?** Develop detailed buyer personas that represent different parts of your target audience. Consider factors similar as age, gender,

position, income position, education, occupation, interests, pursuits, provocations, challenges, and preferred communication channels.

6. **What are your audience segments?** Divide your target audience into distinct segments grounded on demographics, psychographics, actions, interests, or other criteria. This segmentation will help you conform your messaging, content, and marketing strategies to address the specific requirements and preferences of each member.

7. **What platform is suitable for my product?** Choose social media platforms that are most applicable to your target audience. Different platforms attract different demographics and stoner actions, so elect the platforms where your audience is most active and engaged.

8. **Test and Iterate:** Start by targeting a specific audience member with your social media juggernauts and content. Cover the performance of your

juggernauts, track crucial criteria , and gather feedback to assess how well you're reaching and engaging with your target audience. Use this data to upgrade your targeting strategies and acclimate your approach as demanded. By following these tips and strategies, you can effectively choose a target audience for your social media marketing sweats and knitter your messaging and content to reverberate with the right people. Note that audience targeting is an ongoing process, and it's important to continuously dissect data, test, and upgrade your targeting strategies to optimise your social media marketing results.

Setting Clear Goals
In Social Media Marketing, setting clear goals involves defining specific and measurable objects that you aim to achieve through your social media sweats. Clear goals give direction, focus, and a standard for assessing the effectiveness of your social media juggernauts. Then are some crucial aspects of setting clear goals in social media marketing
1. **Be specific:** In particular, your social media goals should be clear, specific, and

well-defined. Avoid vague objects like " increase social media engagement " and rather establish precise objectives similar as " increase Instagram followers by 20 within three months " or " induce 100 leads from Facebook advertisements in a month. "

2. **Measurability:** Your objectives should be measurable so that you can track your progress and estimate the success of your social media juggernauts. Use crucial performance pointers(KPIs) similar as likes, shares, commentary, clicks, transformations, reach, engagement rate, and follower growth to quantify your achievements.

3. **Achievability**: Set realistic objectives that are attainable within your coffers, capabilities, and timeframe. Consider factors like your budget, platoon size, moxie, and competition when establishing your social media objectives . Stretch yourself enough to drive growth, but avoid setting unattainable targets.

4. **Applicability:** Ensure that your social media objectives align with your overall business objects and marketing strategy. Your social media objectives should contribute to broader business objectives similar as adding brand mindfulness, driving website business, boosting deals, or enhancing client engagement.

5. **Time- Bound:** Establish clear timelines and deadlines for achieving your social media objectives . Define specific timeframes for reaching your objects, whether it's daily, yearly, daily, or annually. Setting time- bound objectives creates a sense of urgency and helps you stay focused on negotiating your targets.

6. **Alignment with Strategy:** Your social media objectives should align with your broader marketing strategy and complement other marketing channels and enterprises. Coordinate your social media goals with your overall marketing plan to ensure coherence and consistency across all touchpoints.

7. **Track and Measure:** Implement monitoring and tracking mechanisms to measure progress towards your social media goals. Use analytics tools, reports, dashboards, and metrics to monitor performance, analyze data, and make informed decisions to optimize your social media campaigns.

By setting clear goals in social media marketing, you can establish a roadmap for achieving your objectives, driving engagement, and maximizing the impact of your social media efforts. Clear goals provide focus, accountability, and direction for your social media strategy, helping you measure success and make data-driven decisions to enhance your social media performance.

Define Specific And Measurable Goals
Defining specific and measurable goals for social media involves setting clear objectives that are detailed, quantifiable, and aligned with your business and marketing strategies.
By following these steps, you can define specific and measurable goals for social media that provide clarity, focus, and a roadmap for

achieving success in your social media marketing efforts. Specific and measurable goals help you track progress, measure performance, and make data-driven decisions to enhance the effectiveness of your social media strategy. Here are the key steps to define specific and measurable goals for social media:

1. Identify Key Objectives: Determine the primary goals you want to achieve through social media, such as increasing brand awareness, driving website traffic, generating leads, boosting sales, or improving customer engagement.

2. Make Goals Specific: Clearly define your goals with specific and detailed descriptions. For example, instead of saying "improve engagement," specify "increase engagement rate on Instagram posts by 15% in three months."

3. Ensure Measurability: Establish metrics and key performance indicators (KPIs) that allow you to track and measure progress towards your goals. Use quantifiable metrics like followers, likes, shares, comments, clicks, conversions, reach, engagement rate, or leads generated.

4. Set Realistic Targets: Ensure that your goals are achievable and realistic based on your resources, capabilities, and market conditions. Consider factors like budget, team size, competition, and industry benchmarks when setting your targets.

5. Define Timeframes: Establish clear timelines and deadlines for achieving your goals. Specify the timeframe within which you aim to accomplish your objectives, whether it's weekly, monthly, quarterly, or annually.

6. Align with Strategy: Ensure that your social media goals align with your overall business objectives and marketing strategy. Your social media goals should contribute to broader business goals and complement other marketing channels.

7. Monitor and Adjust: Implement tracking and measurement tools to monitor progress towards your goals. Regularly review performance metrics, analyze data, and make adjustments to optimize your social media strategy and campaigns based on the results.

CHAPTER V

CHOOSING THE RIGHT SOCIAL MEDIA PLATFORMS

Choosing appropriate social media platforms is an important decision for small businesses looking to improve their online image and reach their intended demographic efficiently. With limited resources and time, small businesses must strategically choose platforms that correspond with their brand identity, marketing goals, and audience demographics. Small businesses may improve their social media efforts by understanding the specific features and benefits of each platform, resulting in increased engagement, brand awareness, and, eventually, leads and sales.

Factors To Consider When Choosing Platforms

Target Audience: Take into account the platforms where your target audience is most engaged. By doing this, you can make sure that the correct people are seeing your marketing efforts.

Features & Tools: Seek out platforms with the

features & tools that correspond with your marketing objectives. Pick a platform with a strong advertising system, for instance, if you wish to run advertisements.

Cost: Determine which platform best suits your budget by comparing the costs of using each one. While some sites would not charge a monthly price, others might provide free solutions.

User Base: Take into account the number of users and their demographics on the platform. Wider reach is achieved by having a larger user base, but increased rivalry for attention is possible as well.

Material Type: Certain kinds of material work better on different platforms. For instance, longer textual material might perform better on Facebook or LinkedIn, but photos and videos do better on Instagram.

Brand Image: Take into account the platform's general tone and brand image. Verify that it is consistent with your brand and the message you wish to get over to your target audience.

Statistics and Insights: Seek out platforms that provide statistics and insights so you can monitor the effectiveness of your efforts and modify your approach as necessary.

Integration: Take into account how well the platform works with any other software and resources you might be utilizing for your business.

Time and Resources: Consider how much time and money you have to devote to upkeep and management of your social media presence. Select systems that you can reliably and efficiently operate.

Competition: Look into the existence of your rivals on various platforms and take into account the ones they are effectively utilizing. This might help you determine which platforms would be most advantageous to your business.

An Overview of the Most Widely Used Social Platforms

In order to effectively sell goods and services, small businesses now depend heavily on social media. Thanks to the rapid advancement of technology and the pervasive usage of social media, businesses can now easily reach a larger audience and interact more personally with their customers. But with so many social media sites at their disposal, small businesses may find it difficult to decide which ones are best for their marketing approaches. An overview of the most widely used social media platforms for small business marketing will be given in this article.

Facebook
With more than 2.8 billion active users as of 2021, Facebook is the biggest social media network. It is a feature-rich platform for small businesses, with possibilities for advertising, groups, and business pages among its many offerings. Facebook's vast user base and sophisticated targeting tools make it a great way for businesses to connect and interact with their target market. Additionally, companies can use it to display their goods and services, provide updates and special offers, and engage with

clients directly and through comments and direct messaging.

With facebook, you can expand your business and connect with your preferred clientele thanks to its sizable user base and alternatives for customized advertising. You may sell straight through the platform, interact with your audience through comments and messenger, and share your goods, services, and promotions on your business page. Don't pass up the chance to use Facebook as a social media marketing tool to increase sales and brand awareness.

The Instagram platform

With more than 1 billion active users, Instagram is a very visually appealing platform. It is well-known for emphasizing images and videos, which makes it an excellent platform for companies in the culinary, travel, and fashion industries. Instagram also provides companies with a number of tools, such Instagram Stories, IGTV, and Instagram Shopping, which let them present their goods and services in an eye-catching manner. Businesses can expand their audience and boost brand visibility by utilizing hashtags. Small businesses may effectively utilize Instagram to raise their brand awareness, draw in new clients, and boost sales by consistently publishing high-quality material and implementing strategic marketing techniques.

Twitter

There are more than 330 million active users on the microblogging site Twitter. It's an excellent venue for businesses to disseminate news, promotions, and updates quickly because of its reputation for real-time updates and brief articles. By utilizing hashtags and retweets, companies may expand their audience and have more conversational interactions with them. Additionally, Twitter is a fantastic tool for businesses to answer questions from customers and address grievances.

LinkedIn

With more than 740 million active users, LinkedIn is a professional networking site. For companies in the B2B (business-to-business) sector, it's an excellent way to network with other companies and experts. Additionally, it provides tools like job posts, corporate profiles, and sponsored content, which makes it an excellent platform for companies to market their goods and services and connect with possible partners or customers.

YouTube

Over 2 billion people use the video-sharing website YouTube every day. Video content creation and sharing, including product demos, tutorials, and behind-the-scenes footage, is a great use case for organizations. Through its extensive user base and sophisticated targeting capabilities, companies may expand their brand awareness and connect with a larger market. Additionally, YouTube provides opportunities for advertising, making it an invaluable platform for businesses to promote their products or services.

TikTok

There are more than 1 billion active users on the relatively young platform TikTok. It has become more well-liked among younger audiences and is well-known for its short-form video content. Through influencer relationships or user-generated content, businesses can use TikTok to present their goods and services in an original and entertaining way. But not every business can benefit from TikTok, so before utilizing this platform for marketing, it's important to think about who your target demographic is.

Pinterest

Users of the visual social media site Pinterest can make virtual pinboards to store and exchange ideas, links, and photos. It enables small businesses to access a wide audience and present their goods or services in an eye-catching manner, making it a potent marketing tool. Enterprises can leverage Pinterest to enhance website traffic, elevate brand recognition, and interact with prospective clients. To assist companies in monitoring their success and focusing on particular demographics, it also provides a range of statistics and advertising choices. In general, small businesses can find Pinterest to be a useful and affordable social media marketing tool.

Reddit:

Reddit is a social media conversation and news aggregation platform with more than 430 million members. Users can post and discuss a range of topics within the communities, or subreddits, that make up the platform. Reddit is a well-liked forum where users can locate specialized groups and have discussions about a variety of subjects.

Snapchat:
With over 500 million active users, Snapchat is a messaging app. Being a well-liked medium for lighthearted content sharing and informal contact, it is well-known for its vanishing messages and filters. Businesses can build sponsored filters and lenses on Snapchat and advertise using its features.

In conclusion, the objectives, target market, and sector of the business all play a role in selecting the best social media channels for small business marketing. Before selecting which platforms to employ, it is crucial to investigate and comprehend the features and target audience of each. Through the appropriate use of social media platforms, small businesses may connect and interact with their target market more successfully, build brand awareness, and eventually boost sales and expansion.

CHAPTER VI

IDENTIFYING THE TARGET AUDIENCE FOR YOUR SMALL BUSINESS

Choosing the right target audience for your social media marketing could be tasking and complicated especially when it has to do with a small business. To do this effectively and efficiently, you have to follow precisely all the way as outlined in this chapter. It's essential to start by having a clear understanding of your business, products, and services. Identify your unique selling points, value proposition, and the benefits you offer to guests. This understanding will help you determine who would be interested in what you have to offer.

What are your goals?

Determine your social media marketing goals and objects. Are you looking to increase brand mindfulness, drive website business, induce leads, boost deals, or enhance client engagement? Your objectives will impact the type of audience you target and the messaging you use. The most pivotal aspect of any social media strategy is to set S.M.A.R.T.(Specific,

Measureable, Attainable, Realistic, and Timely) social media marketing objectives. Advertising blindly and awaiting to achieve massive quantities of new deals would be like cooking without the right ingredients and awaiting great taste. By setting objectives before you begin, it's easier to measure social media success or failure. These social media objectives are not always concentrated on money or return on investment, and they should not be. Social media marketing is further about engagement with your target audience and furnishing results to problems rather than just selling . Successful brands produce inbound marketing openings and educate vs sell.

Goals of Social Media Marketing

1. Brand mindfulness.
2. Enhance Public Relations.
3. Build Community of lawyers
4. Research and Development
5. Driving Deals and Leads

There's a need to look at your current client base and assess their demographics, psychographics, actions, and preferences. Collecting data and perceptivity similar to common characteristics, interests, requirements, and pain points about your target audience through colorful platforms can help your small business to understand the overall audience demographics and brand sentiment. exercising social media in request exploration.

For improved, measurable results, the below basic steps offer easy to implement ways to utilize social media in your market research methods

Track Trends with Social Media for Real-Time insight Most social media platforms, similar to Twitter or Facebook, offer multiple ways to dissect trends and conduct request exploration. Simply search the rearmost posts and popular terms, to gain sapience into rising trends and see what guests are talking about in real- time. For example, many hashtag searches on Twitter relating to your brand, assiduity or product can be conducted and instant announcements entered when clients or competitors use crucial terms.

Learn the Language of Your Audience for Improved Marketing Appeal: The words and factors that you use to track the success of your product or business might not always align with what guests find most important. By assaying social media exchanges about your product or service, you can learn what factors guests use to determine value as well as the way that they speak about your product, service or brand. By exercising these factors and terms within your own marketing, you can speak directly to consumers and ameliorate the effectiveness of your marketing sweats. By creating client-centric delineations of value, quality and other important terms, you can help to produce a brand or product image that's unique amongst challengers and speaks directly to your target request.

Use the Real- Time Aspects of Social Media for Quick Research: Traditional request disquisition styles, analogous as checks or study groups, could take months to plan, form and execute. With social media, disquisition can be conducted in a matter of beats or hours. This makes it possible to use request disquisition to follow increasingly specific aspects of your marketing sweats. From product launches to follow- up marketing, each part of your marketing plan can be analyzed independently for better results across the wholeness of your marketing plan. rather than spending months developing a marketing disquisition plan, and possibly only gaining outdated information as trends change, you can use social media for request disquisition right now.

Use Social Media to Broaden the Compass of Your Market Research: Social media broadens the compass of request disquisition by furnishing access to vast amounts of real- time data and perceptivity from a different range of stoners. Through social media platforms, businesses can gather information on consumer preferences, conduct, and trends, allowing for further targeted and substantiated marketing strategies. Also, social media enables companies to engage directly with their target cult, gather feedback, and cover brand sentiment, ultimately enhancing the effectiveness of request exploration efforts.The casual nature and easy access of social media also helps to promote user commerce, engagement and participation. This improves the chances of carrying useful, accurate and honest data from your sweats.

Discover Unnoticed Trends and perceptivity by Engaging rather than Leading: One of the biggest weaknesses to most marketing research methods is that they are driven by questions. To obtain the proper information, you must first know what to ask. At the same time, simply rewording a question can result in dramatically different answers. This means that your market research is only as good as your questions. With the broad scope and interactive nature of social media, information is gained through interaction and observation. Instead of leading the discussions, you can simply observe or join in as an equal. This can result in a variety of answers and discoveries that might have remained hidden using other research methods.

Harness Social Media Research for Improved Cost effectiveness: In utmost cases, exercising social media for request disquisition is simply a matter of investing time. Free tools live for nearly every social media platform to help gather information and use it to decide useful information. When compared to focus panels, discussion groups, studies and checks, the cost difference is stunning. Through user engagement and discussion, your social media disquisition also serves as advertising, brand structure, network structure, preeminent generation and offers numerous other advancements for your business or brand. When planned and executed properly, numerous request disquisition tools offer the cost effectiveness and overall benefit of social media disquisition.

From reduced costs and real- time access to information to the capability to uncover retired trends and improve your marketing approach, social media offers important ways to optimize the request disquisitions of any business. Stylish of all, social media disquisition offers numerous ways to interact with your request and make your business. Conducting disquisition is as simple as subscribing up for a social media service, analogous as LinkedIn or Twitter, and exercising their erected- in quest features. Within beats, your business can start assaying trends, perfecting your marketing strategies and work

Creating a social media marketing strategy
1. Set clear objectives . Setting clear objectives and strategies for social media marketing is essential for success. Some pivotal ways to consider include defining specific and measurable objects, relating your target cult, concluding the right social media platforms, creating engaging content, establishing a harmonious announcement schedule, covering

and assaying performance criteria, and conforming strategies as demanded to optimize results. By setting clear objectives and administering a well- allowed - eschewal strategy, you can effectively reach and engage your target cult on social media.

2. Research your buyer personas and audience. Probing buyer personas and understanding your target audience is indeed a vital strategy for social media marketing success. A detailed buyer personas that represent different corridors of your target audience. Consider factors analogous as age, gender, position, income position, education, occupation, interests, hobbies, provocations, challenges, and preferred communication channels. By creating detailed buyer personas, you can more confirm your content, messaging, and advertising efforts to resonate with your target cult's conditions, preferences, and conduct. This targeted approach can help increase engagement, drive metamorphoses, and make stronger connections with your cult on social media platforms. Conducting thorough disquisition on buyer personas and cult demographics can give precious perceptivity that inform your social media marketing strategies and ultimately lead to farther effective and poignant campaigns.

3. Determine which social platforms you 'll market on. Choose social media platforms that are most applicable to your target cult. Different platforms attract different demographics and user conduct, so handpick the platforms where your cult is most active and engaged. It's important to consider factors analogous as your target cult demographics, preferences, and behavior , as well as the nature of your products or services. Different social media platforms feed to different user demographics and offer unique features and functionalities. By concluding the platforms where your target cult is most active and engaged, you can maximize the reach and impact of your social media marketing sweats. Conducting disquisition and assaying data can help you identify the most suitable platforms for your brand and develop adapted strategies to effectively engage with your cult on those platforms.

4. Establish your most important metrics and KPIs.
Establishing key performance indicators (KPIs) and metrics is crucial for measuring the effectiveness of your social media marketing

efforts. By defining clear objectives and identifying the most relevant metrics to track, such as engagement rates, click-through rates, conversion rates, and follower growth, you can assess the performance of your campaigns and make data-driven decisions to optimize your strategies. Monitoring and analyzing these metrics regularly can provide valuable insights into the impact of your social media marketing activities, help you identify areas for improvement, and guide future decision-making to achieve your marketing goals. Establishing meaningful KPIs and metrics is essential for evaluating the success of your social media marketing efforts and ensuring a positive return on investment.

5. Get to know your competition.
Knowing your competition is a valuable aspect of developing a strong social media marketing strategy. By conducting competitive analysis, you can gain insights into what strategies and tactics are working for your competitors, identify gaps or opportunities in the market, and differentiate your brand from others in the industry. Understanding your competition's social media presence, content strategy, engagement tactics, and audience demographics

can help you refine your own approach, benchmark your performance, and stay ahead in the competitive landscape. By leveraging competitive insights, you can make informed decisions, refine your messaging, and optimize your social media marketing efforts to effectively position your brand and drive success.

6. Create unique and engaging content.
Creating unique and engaging content is a key component of successful social media marketing. By developing content that is original, relevant, and valuable to your target audience, you can capture their attention, spark interest, and encourage interaction and sharing. Unique and engaging content helps differentiate your brand, establish credibility, and build relationships with your audience on social media platforms. It is important to understand your audience's preferences, interests, and needs, and tailor your content to resonate with them. Incorporating visual elements, storytelling, interactive features, and user-generated content can also enhance the engagement and effectiveness of your social media marketing efforts. By consistently delivering high-quality and compelling content, you can attract and

retain followers, drive traffic, and achieve your marketing goals on social media.

7. Organize a schedule for your posts.

Organizing a schedule for your posts is a key component of an effective social media marketing strategy. By establishing a consistent posting schedule, you can maintain a regular presence on social media platforms, keep your audience engaged, and build brand awareness. Planning and scheduling posts in advance can also help you maintain a cohesive content strategy, ensure timely delivery of messages, and optimize engagement by posting at times when your audience is most active. Additionally, scheduling posts allows you to allocate time for creating high-quality content, monitoring performance metrics, and adjusting your strategy based on data insights. Overall, organizing a schedule for your posts is essential for maximizing the impact of your social media marketing efforts and achieving your marketing goals.

8. Review and adjust your strategy.

Reviewing and adjusting your social media marketing strategy in response to growth is a key practice to ensure continued success and effectiveness. As your brand and audience evolve, it is important to regularly assess the performance of your social media campaigns, analyze key metrics and data, and identify areas for improvement or optimization. By monitoring growth indicators such as engagement rates, follower growth, website traffic, and conversion rates, you can gain valuable insights into the effectiveness of your current strategy and make informed decisions on adjustments or refinements. Adapting your strategy based on growth trends and performance data can help you stay competitive, reach your marketing goals, and maintain a strong presence on social media platforms.

CHAPTER VII

TOOLS TO HELP YOU CHOOSE A TARGET AUDIENCE FOR SOCIAL MEDIA MARKETING

Loomly: Loomly stands out for its stoner-friendly interface and cooperative approach to social media scheduling. This platform facilitates cooperation, allowing multiple druggies to contribute to content creation and scheduling. With a focus on effectiveness, Loomly empowers druggies to plan, produce, and publish content seamlessly.

Sendible: For those seeking a comprehensive social media operation result, Sendible proves to be a precious supporter. This platform offers a centralized hub for scheduling posts, covering engagement, and assaying performance across colorful social media channels. Its intuitive dashboard and analytics tools make it a go- to choice for businesses aiming to optimize their online strategies.

Birdseye: Birdseye takes a unique approach by furnishing a visual content timetable. This platform's raspberry's- eye view simplifies the process of planning and organizing social media content. With its emphasis on visual representation, Birdseye aims to enhance the stoner's capability to map and execute juggernauts with perfection.

Planory: Planory steps into the scene with a focus on simplicity and effectiveness. This platform is designed to streamline the planning and scheduling of social media posts. Its minimalist interface hides a important machine that enables druggies to organize content painlessly, making it an ideal choice for those who value straightforward yet effective social media operation.

Brand24: Monitoring and managing your brand's online character becomes flawless with Brand24. This platform goes beyond scheduling posts and delves into real- time shadowing of social media mentions. By furnishing perceptivity into brand mentions and sentiment analysis, Brand24 equips druggies with the tools demanded to engage with their audience proactively. Heyorca Collaboration takes center stage with Heyorca. This platform focuses on easing cooperation among happy generators, allowing for flawless collaboration on social media juggernauts.

Heyorca: Collaboration takes center stage with Heyorca. This platform focuses on facilitating teamwork among content creators, allowing for seamless collaboration on social media campaigns. Heyorca's workflow management tools and communication features empower teams to work together efficiently, ensuring that every aspect of social media strategy is coordinated effectively.

Agorapulse: Agorapulse is a social media operation tool that enables druggies to record posts, cover social channels, and engage with their audience. It provides analytics to track performance and collaboration features for brigades.

Iconosquare: Iconosquare specializes in Instagram analytics and operation. It offers perceptivity into engagement, audience growth, and hashtag performance. Druggies can record posts and track their Instagram presence.

PromoRepublic: PromoRepublic is a social media marketing platform with a focus on content creation. It provides templates for social media posts, scheduling options, and analytics to optimize content strategy.

Audience: audience is a social media analytics tool designed to help druggies understand and dissect their followers. It provides perceptivity into demographics, engagement criteria , and helps upgrade content strategies grounded on audience preferences.

Napoleoncat: Napoleoncat is a social media operation and analytics tool. It offers features like social media scheduling, contender analysis, and in- depth reporting to optimize social media performance.

Visime: Visime is a visual content creation tool, allowing druggies to produce engaging plates and illustrations for social media. It focuses on simplicity and effectiveness in the design process.

Buffer: Buffer is a popular social media operation platform. It facilitates post scheduling, analytics, and platoon collaboration. druggies can manage multiple social media accounts from a centralized dashboard.

Pablo: Pablo is a tool by Buffer designed for creating engaging images for social media posts. It provides easy- to- use templates and features to enhance visual content. ContentCal ContentCal is a cooperative content planning platform. It streamlines the content creation process, aids in scheduling posts, and offers analytics for performance shadowing.

Sprout Social: Sprout Social is a comprehensive social media operation and analytics tool. It covers scheduling, engagement, analytics, and social listening to give a holistic approach to social media strategy.

Followerwonk: Followerwonk, owned by Moz, focuses on Twitter analytics. It helps users analyze followers, find influencers, and optimize their Twitter strategy for better engagement.Tailwind: Tailwind is a social media scheduling tool with a strong emphasis on Pinterest and Instagram. It offers features like scheduling posts, analytics, and optimizing content strategy.

Onlypult: Onlypult is a social media scheduling tool that supports various platforms. It allows users to plan and schedule posts in advance, ensuring a consistent social media presence.

Later: Later is a visual content scheduling tool, primarily used for Instagram. It provides features for scheduling posts, managing content, and analyzing performance metrics.

Tagboard: Tagboard is a social media monitoring and analytics tool that aggregates content from various social media platforms based on specific hashtags. It allows users to track trends, monitor conversations, and gather insights about specific topics or events.

BuzzSumo: BuzzSumo is a content discovery and social media analytics platform that helps users identify trending topics, analyze content performance, and find influencers in their niche. It provides valuable insights for content strategy and social media marketing campaigns.

Mention: Mention is a media monitoring tool that tracks mentions of a brand, keyword, or topic across the web and social media platforms. It helps users monitor their online reputation, track competitors, and engage with their audience in real-time.

Emplify: Emplify is an employee engagement platform that helps organizations measure and improve employee satisfaction, productivity, and performance. It provides insights through surveys, analytics, and actionable recommendations to enhance workplace culture and productivity.

Tweepi: Tweepi is a Twitter management tool that helps users manage their Twitter accounts more effectively. It offers features for managing followers, identifying inactive accounts, and finding relevant users to follow or engage with.

Feedly: Feedly is a content aggregator and RSS reader that allows users to follow their favorite websites, blogs, and publications in one place. It helps users stay updated on industry news, trends, and relevant content for content curation and research purposes.

Lumen5: Lumen5 is a video creation platform that helps users turn text-based content into engaging videos. It uses AI and machine learning algorithms to automate the video creation process, making it easier for users to create professional-looking videos for social media and marketing campaigns.

Zapier: Zapier is an automation tool that connects different apps and services to automate repetitive tasks and workflows. It allows users to create custom integrations, or "Zaps," between various apps without writing any code, saving time and increasing productivity.

Canva: Canva is a graphic design platform that allows users to create a wide range of visual content, including social media graphics, presentations, posters, and more. It offers a user-friendly interface with drag-and-drop functionality, along with a vast library of templates, images, and design elements.

SocialPilot: SocialPilot is a social media management tool that enables users to schedule posts, analyze performance, and manage multiple social media accounts from a single dashboard. It offers features such as content scheduling, social media analytics, team collaboration, and client management.

eClincher: eClincher is a social media management platform that helps users manage, schedule, and analyze their social media accounts. It offers features such as content publishing, social media monitoring, engagement, and analytics, along with tools for team collaboration and content curation.

Hootsuite: Hootsuite is a popular social media management platform that allows users to schedule posts, monitor social media activity, and analyze performance across multiple social networks. It offers features such as content scheduling, social media listening, analytics, and team collaboration.

Social Champ: Social Champ is a social media management tool that helps users schedule posts, analyze performance, and automate repetitive tasks across various social media platforms. It offers features such as content scheduling, social media analytics, RSS feeds integration, and team collaboration.

Zoho Social: Zoho Social is a social media management platform that enables users to manage multiple social media accounts, schedule posts, monitor mentions, and analyze performance. It offers features such as content scheduling, social media analytics, CRM integration, and team collaboration.

Tailwind: Tailwind can be a powerful tool for social media marketing due to its ability to streamline the design process and create visually appealing content efficiently.

Here's how Tailwind can be utilized:

1.Design Consistency: Tailwind's utility-first approach ensures consistent design across social media platforms. By using predefined classes, marketers can maintain a cohesive brand identity in their posts.

2. Efficient Workflow: With Tailwind, marketers can quickly create and modify designs without writing custom CSS. This speed and efficiency allow for faster content creation and posting, crucial in the fast-paced world of social media.

3. Responsive Design: Tailwind's responsive utilities make it easy to create content optimized for various screen sizes, ensuring that posts look great on desktop, mobile, and tablet devices.

4. Scheduling and Analytics: Tailwind offers features for scheduling posts in advance and analyzing their performance. Marketers can schedule posts at optimal times for their audience and track metrics to refine their social media strategy.

5. Community and Collaboration: Tailwind provides a platform for marketers to connect with others in their industry, share insights, and collaborate on content. This community aspect can lead to valuable networking opportunities and shared learning experiences.

Overall, Tailwind serves as a valuable tool for social media marketers by streamlining the design process, maintaining consistency, and offering features for scheduling and analytics.

CHAPTER VIII

BUILDING YOUR ONLINE PRESENCE ON SOCIAL MEDIA

A. Creating Social Media Profiles and Cover Photo

Creating Social Media Profiles

Profile Picture and Cover Photo: When a potential customer visits a business's social media profile, they frequently notice these visual components first. They aid in giving the brand a visual identity and increase its recognition. Users are more likely to explore a business further if their profile picture and cover photo are visually appealing and create a positive first impression.

Bio/About Section: In this section, the business's values, goods, and services should be briefly described. This enables prospective clients to rapidly comprehend the nature of the business and its offerings. Establishing the tone and personality of the brand through a well-written bio can also help the target audience relate to the brand more.

Contact Details: It is simpler for clients to get in touch with a firm when contact details, such as an email address, phone number, and website link, are included in the profile. In addition to increasing sales and inquiries, this can help you gain the confidence and respect of your clients.

B. Branding Your Profiles
Consistent Visuals: A unified and identifiable brand may be produced by using consistent visuals, such as color schemes, typefaces, and photos, throughout all social media profiles. Customers will also find it simpler to recognize your business across various platforms because of this uniformity.

Tone and Voice: It's critical to keep your tone and voice the same in all consumer interactions and social media posts. This makes the brand more relatable and helps to define its identity.

Hashtags: Using hashtags can help a business's social media posts get more attention and be found by potential customers. Adding well-chosen and pertinent hashtags to the business's profile might also aid in growing its following.

C. Tips for Optimizing Profiles

Employ Keywords: Relevant keywords can assist increase a business's visibility on social media and increase the number of potential customers who find it by being included in the bio, about section, and posts.

Keep Information Updated: To guarantee accuracy and prevent customer confusion, it's critical to routinely update the profile information, including contact information, website links, and business hours.

Interact with Followers: Using social media to interact and engage with followers helps strengthen ties with clients and boost brand loyalty. Another way for a firm to demonstrate its appreciation for its clients is by replying to reviews, mails, and comments.

CHAPTER IX
CREATING ENGAGING CONTENT

Social media is getting a pivotal element of any business's marketing plan, anyhow of size. Social media has millions of active druggies across several platforms, making it an effective tool for connecting and interacting with new guests. But with such important content available on social media, it can be delicate for businesses to stand out and attract the interest of their target audience. Then is where intriguing stuff comes into play. Any form of material that draws observers in, stimulates discussion, and motivates them to partake it with others is considered engaging content. Having a strong brand presence, raising brand recognition, and ultimately driving deals are all made possible by it, which makes it pivotal for social media marketing. The types of material that can prop in achieving social media marketing objectives and the reasons why engaging content is essential are bandied below.

A. Importance of Engaging Content
   The creation of catchy
   content is essential to small businesses'

success with social media marketing. Social media has developed into a potent tool in moment's digital geography that helps businesses connect and interact with their target audience. Due to the fact that millions of people use social media platforms daily, businesses have a special chance to present their brand and establish a connection with implicit guests.

For small businesses using social media marketing, the following are some reasons why producing catchy content is important.

Attracts Attention: It's critical to produce material on social media that stands out and draws druggies in, especially with the violent competition. intriguing pictures, eye-catching images, and interactive pates are exemplifications of engaging content that can draw in new observers and raise brand mindfulness.

Developing Brand Identity: Businesses can forge a strong online presence on social media by regularly publishing intriguing material. Businesses can demonstrate their own personality, beliefs, and charge by producing content that speaks to their target audience. This helps to cultivate a devoted following.

Increases Engagement: Engaging content encourages druggies to interact with a brand's social media runner, performing in increased engagement. This can include likes, commentary, shares, and click- through to the business's website. The further engagement a post receives, the more it'll be shown to other druggies, adding the reach of the content.

1. Increases transformations For small businesses, engaging content can also affect increased conversion rates. Businesses may develop credibility and trust with their audience by producing content that adds value. This can ultimately affect transformations and deals.
2. Promotes stoner- Generated information intriguing information might motivate compendiums to write original papers about a company or item. For businesses, stoner-generated content is extremely useful since it can reach a larger audience through shares and mentions, and it acts as social evidence.
3. Fosters connections The main thing of social media is to establish a fellowship with druggies. By interacting and connecting with their audience through engaging content,

businesses can produce a sense of community and establish enduring connections with their guests.

In conclusion, producing intriguing content is essential for small businesses using social media marketing since it fosters stoner-generated content creation, attention- getting, brand identity development, engagement, transformations, and client connections. In the Machiavellian realm of social media marketing, it's a necessary tool for companies to separate themselves and thrive

B. Different Social Media Content Types:

Images and Graphics

In comparison to text-only information, visual content is generally more engaging and memorable. Users' attention can be swiftly captured by images and visuals, which can also elicit strong feelings or a message. Infographics, memes, and behind-the-scenes photos are a few examples of what they can include. Having visually attractive and high-quality photographs and graphics can assist build a strong brand identity and boost social media engagement.

Videos:

For good reason, videos have grown in

fashionability on social media spots. They can cover a lot of ground snappily and with great engagement. videos can include behind- the- scenes footage, client witnesses, product demonstrations, and indeed educational and entertaining content. They're an effective fashion for social media marketing since they've the eventuality to go viral and reach a wider audience.

User-Generated Content
User- Generated Content A user- generated piece of content is any content that they've developed, including social media bulletins, reviews, or witnesses that punctuate the goods or services of a brand. Because it's regarded as objective and real, it's veritably good at establishing credibility and trust with prospective guests. Publicizing stoner- generated material on social media can inspire other druggies to produce and circulate their own content, thereby boosting commerce and brand recognition.

Contests and Giveaways
Holding contests and giveaways is a terrific method to spark interest and participation on social media. They may take the kind of photo or

video competitions, in which participants are urged to produce and distribute brand-related content. Giveaways and contests boost participation and broaden the brand's audience because participants frequently tag friends and family.

C. Writing Interesting Content:

Know Your Audience: Knowing your target audience is the first step in producing interesting content. Understanding their preferences, hobbies, and demographics will help you create material that appeals to them. Performing market research and examining social media data can offer insightful information about the behavior of your target audience and assist in producing relevant and engaging content.

Make Use of pictures: As was already established, pictures are incredibly captivating and can grab an audience's attention fast. To increase the appeal and shareability of your social media postings, include high-quality photos and videos. But pay attention to the platform's rules and make sure the images are adjusted for various screen sizes.

Be Real: In social media marketing, being real is essential. Consumers may become suspicious of a brand if they perceive information to be unduly promotional or fraudulent. When posting on social media, be sincere and open, and establish a personal connection with your followers. This can promote brand loyalty and help establish a solid relationship.

Make Use of Hashtags: Hashtags are a useful tool for expanding the audience for and exposure of your postings on social media. To increase the discoverability of your material and expand its readership, use trending and relevant hashtags. But be careful—using too many hashtags can make your content appear spammy and reduce interaction.

Promote User engagement: Producing visually beautiful postings is only one aspect of engaging content; another is promoting user engagement. Pose queries, conduct polls, or make interactive postings that invite visitors to leave remarks or tag friends. This can foster a feeling of community around your brand in addition to raising engagement.

To sum it up, interesting content is essential for

social media marketing since it makes companies stand out, have a strong online presence, and eventually increase sales. Businesses may develop an efficient social media marketing plan that successfully engages their target audience by utilizing a variety of content kinds and according to these guidelines.

CHAPTER X

GROWING YOUR FOLLOWING

The success of any brand or business on social media depends on having a large following. It gives you a direct channel of communication with your target market, enabling you to interact and develop connections with possible clients. Along with raising sales and conversion rates, a large following also boosts a brand's credibility and visibility. As such, it is imperative that you consistently expand and cultivate your social media following.

A. The Value of a Large Following

Having a large following is essential for social media marketing because it increases the visibility and interaction of your material. You can strengthen your brand messaging, raise brand awareness, and improve traffic to your website or items when you have a sizable and active audience. Having a large following also helps you become more credible and authoritative in your field, which makes it simpler to draw in new clients and cultivate enduring connections with your current ones. A sizable following also gives you important information about the tastes and habits of your target market, which you can use to better target your marketing efforts and content. All things considered, having a sizable social media following is essential to the success of your marketing initiatives.

B. Strategies for Growing Your Following

There are several strategies you can employ to grow your following on social media marketing:

Consistent and High-quality Content: Publish high-quality content on a regular basis that appeals to, engages, and is relevant to your target audience. They will be inspired to follow you and tell others about your material as a result.

Make Use of Hashtags: To expand your audience and improve visibility, look up and incorporate pertinent hashtags into your postings. Hashtags make your material easier to find for visitors to find and can draw in new followers who are interested in the subjects you write about.

Interact with Your Audience: Instantaneously reply to messages, remarks, and mentions. Interacting with your audience fosters a sense of community and demonstrates your appreciation for their opinions. To promote meaningful encounters, ask questions, start conversations, and get feedback.

Work with Influencers: Getting together with influential people in your field will help you establish credibility and showcase your business to their following. Influencers have the power to spread the word about your products or content, expanding your audience and drawing in new fans.

Cross-Promote on Other Platforms: Spread the word about your social media accounts via email newsletters, your website, and other online profiles. By using cross-promotion, you can take advantage of your current audiences and encourage them to follow you across other media.

Hold Giveaways and Contests: Plan giveaways or contests where entry requires followers on your social media pages. This might create discussion about your business and encourage others to follow you.

Paid Advertising: Take into account making an investment in social media platform paid advertising. You may reach a larger audience and draw in followers who are actually interested in your products or content with the use of targeted advertisements.

Analyze and Optimize: Using analytics tools, evaluate your social media performance on a regular basis. Determine the content that your audience finds engaging and adjust your approach accordingly. With the use of this data-driven strategy, you may improve your strategies and gain more followers.

Keep in mind that expanding your fan base requires time and work. Maintaining consistency, interacting with your audience, and offering value are crucial for creating a devoted and active community.

C. Tracking and Measuring Growth

Monitoring and measuring the growth of your social media following is crucial for determining which techniques are effective and which ones require improvement. The majority of social networking sites provide analytics tools that let you monitor interaction rates, follower counts, and other pertinent data. You may determine what kinds of material and tactics are most effective for your audience by examining this data, and you can then modify your strategy appropriately. This will assist you in reaching your social media objectives and expanding your fan base.

CHAPTER XI

ENGAGING AND BUILDING RELATIONSHIPS WITH YOUR AUDIENCE

Developing and sustaining relationships with your audience is one of the most important aspects of any successful marketing strategy, and social media has become an essential element of it. Building a feeling of community and real connections with your audience on social media is just as important as marketing your business. Here are some efficient methods for interacting with and forming connections with your audience on social media:

A. Replying to Messages and Comments

Answering messages and comments from your audience is one of the most crucial methods to interact with them. Whether it's a compliment, a query, or a grievance, taking the time to recognize and reply to your audience demonstrates that you respect and are aware of their opinions.

B. Organizing Live Streams and Q&A Sessions

One of the best ways to interact with your audience in real time on social media is to host Q&A sessions and live streaming. This enables them to communicate with you and other community members, exchange ideas, and ask questions. It also allows you to show off your knowledge, clear up any misunderstandings or worries, and establish a closer bond with your audience.

C. Promoting Content Created by Users

Any content about your brand that is produced by your audience is known as user-generated content, or UGC. Reviews, pictures, videos, and more can be included in this. User-generated content (UGC) is an effective means of interacting with your audience since it lets you display testimonials and real-life experiences in addition to demonstrating that people are talking about your business. Using branded hashtags, holding competitions, or just asking your audience to share their brand experiences are all ways to promote user-generated content (UGC).

D. Using Social Media to Improve Customer Support

Customer service can also benefit greatly from the use of social media. A lot of people use social media to ask inquiries or voice concerns, so it's critical to keep an eye on these platforms and reply as soon as possible. You may transform unpleasant encounters into positive ones and demonstrate to your audience that you are concerned about their happiness by offering exceptional customer service on social media.

In conclusion, the success of your marketing initiatives depends on your ability to interact and establish a rapport with your audience on social media. You may build a robust and devoted community around your brand by answering messages and comments, holding Q&A sessions and live streaming, supporting user-generated content, and using social media for customer support. Your social media marketing efforts will benefit if you always remember to be responsive, real, and sincere in your interactions with your audience.

CHAPTER XII

LEVERAGING SOCIAL MEDIA FOR SALES AND CONVERSION

Using social media for deals and conversion includes establishing brand mindfulness, communicating with implicit guests, and eventually adding deals. Using targeted advertising, interesting content creation, and follower engagement, businesses can effectively reach their target demographic and win them over as pious guests. Using social media for product and service creation, consumer feedback, and connection structure can increase deals and transformations

The following list of best practices includes how to use social media to increase sales and conversions:

Know Your Audience: Knowing your target audience is the first step in using social media to increase sales and conversions. This covers their internet activities, hobbies, and demographics. You may use this information to better target your messaging and content so that people can interact with it and find you.

Produce Captivating material: Creating interesting and high-quality material is essential to drawing in readers and encouraging them to make a purchase. This can contain eye-catching pictures and videos, instructional and interesting articles, and interactive elements like surveys and quizzes.

Communicate with Your Audience: Social media is a platform for two-way conversation. It's critical to interact with your audience on a proactive basis by answering messages, comments, and mentions. This not only fosters a relationship with your audience but also demonstrates your appreciation for their comments and viewpoints.

Make Use of Social Media Advertising: With the growth in algorithm modifications and the decline in organic reach on social media, paid advertising may be a very successful strategy for expanding your audience and increasing conversions. You may reach your targeted audience by using the many targeting tools available on social media sites like Facebook, Instagram, and LinkedIn.

Monitor and Evaluate Your activities: In order to determine what is effective and what needs to be improved, it is imperative that you routinely monitor and evaluate your social media activities. Metrics like interaction, website traffic, and conversions can be tracked as part of this. Make educated judgments using this information, then modify your plan of action accordingly.

Importance of Social Media for Sales

Social media has become into a vital tool for companies looking to connect and interact with their target market. With more than 3.6 billion members globally, social media sites like Facebook, Instagram, and Twitter offer businesses access to a sizable potential consumer base.

Because consumers are spending more time on social media platforms and using them to study products and services before making a purchase, social media marketing has become more and more significant. Actually, according to a PwC survey, 37% of consumers use social media to research goods and services before making a purchase.

Social media also makes it possible for companies to communicate directly with their clients, giving them a special chance to establish rapport and credibility with their target market.

Strategies for Driving Sales through Social Media

1. Special Offers and Rebates
   Using discounts and promotions is one of the best methods to use social media to increase sales. Creating unique promo codes or launching time-limited promotions on social networking sites are two ways to accomplish this. Customers are encouraged to act swiftly because this not only creates a sense of urgency but also incentivizes them to make a purchase.

2. Direct Marketing
   Sales can be significantly increased by working with social media influencers who have a sizable following and following. Businesses can expand their audience and gain followers' trust by collaborating with relevant influencers.

Sales may eventually rise as a result of this raising brand awareness.

3. User-Generated Content: Content produced by a brand's customers or followers is referred to as user-generated content (UGC). Posting user-generated content (UGC) to social media platforms not only demonstrates a brand's genuineness but also motivates users to interact with the material and even make a purchase. Reposting client testimonials, images, or videos that highlight your business' goods or services is one way to achieve this.

4. Ads that Retarget
Businesses can target people who have previously connected with their brand on social media by using retargeting advertising. Businesses can remind these users of goods or services they have expressed interest in and persuade them to buy by displaying relevant advertisements to them.

Measuring ROI and Conversions:
It's critical to monitor and measure important indicators to ascertain how well social media activities are generating sales and conversions. These can include click-through rates on social media postings, conversions from social media campaigns, and traffic to websites derived from social media.

It's imperative to evaluate the return on investment(ROI) of social media trials by differing the charges incurred in social media marketing with the earnings deduced from those trials. When measuring ROI in social media marketing, businesses generally follow a structured approach to dissect the fiscal impact of their social media efforts.

Below is a detailed explanation of how ROI in social media marketing is measured
1. Define objectives and objects before measuring ROI, it's essential to establish clear objectives and objects for your social media marketing juggernauts. These objectives could include adding brand mindfulness, driving website business, generating leads, or boosting deals.

2. Track crucial performance pointers(KPIs) Identify and track crucial performance pointers that align with your objectives . Common KPIs in social media marketing include engagement criteria (likes, shares, commentary), conversion rate, client accession cost, and client continuance value.
3. Calculate costs Determine the costs associated with your social media marketing sweats, including charges for content creation, advertising, social media operation tools, and hand hires devoted to social media conditioning.
4. Measure profit generated Track the profit generated as a result of your social media marketing juggernauts. This could include direct deals attributed to social media, leads generated, or client accessions.
5. Calculate ROI: To calculate ROI, use the following formula:
   ROI = (Revenue generated - Cost of social media marketing) / Cost of social media marketing.
6. Analyze results: Evaluate the ROI of your social media marketing campaigns to determine their effectiveness. Compare the ROI of different campaigns, channels,

or strategies to identify what is working well and where improvements can be made.
7. Adjust strategies: Based on the ROI analysis, make data-driven decisions to optimize your social media marketing strategies. Allocate resources to high-performing campaigns, refine targeting and messaging, and experiment with new tactics to improve ROI over time.

By following these steps and continuously monitoring and analyzing the performance of your social media marketing efforts, you can effectively measure and improve the ROI of your social media campaigns.

CHAPTER XIII

MONITORING AND ANALYZING YOUR SOCIAL MEDIA PERFORMANCE

Businesses aiming to maximize their marketing sweats and enhance their online presence must nearly cover and assess their social media performance. Businesses are suitable to gain important perceptivity into the efficacy of their social media enterprise by covering important pointers and examining data from social media platforms. This procedure entails tracking criteria like prints, click-through rates, conversion rates, engagement rates, and reach in order to estimate how social media sweats affect audience engagement and eventually lead to transformations. Businesses can use this data to dissect trends, assess the effectiveness of their social media juggernauts, and make well-informed opinions to raise their overall performance on social media.

A. The Value of Monitoring and Examining Data

Social media is becoming a pivotal element of any business's marketing strategy in the digital age. Millions of people use social media, thus it's critical for businesses to be present on these platforms and keep a close eye on their performance. You can make wise opinions to enhance your approach by keeping an eye on and assessing data, which can offer perceptive information about how well your social media marketing enterprise is working.

B. Key Metrics to Monitor

Engagement: Engagement Likes, commentary, shares, and clicks on your content fall under this order. A high chance of commerce suggests that your material is connected with compendiums and has the implication to broaden your audience's exposure and brand recognition.Reach This index indicates how numerous people view your composition. Monitoring reach is pivotal to knowing how far your social media juggernauts are spreading and whether they're connecting with your intended audience.

Follower growth: Monitoring your number of followers will help you understand how your audience is expanding over time. A harmonious

rise in followers is a sign that your content is drawing in new bones
and keeping the bones
you formerly have

The amount of clicks on a link or call-to-action (CTA) in your post is measured by the click-through rate (CTR). A high conversion rate (CTR) indicates that your content is interesting and brings visitors to your landing page or website.

Conversion rate: This indicator indicates the proportion of website visitors that complete the targeted action, such buying something or submitting a form. Monitoring your conversion rate can assist you in determining how well your social media marketing efforts are converting users into leads.

Monitoring and Analyzing Tools For Social Media Performance
1. Social media analytics platforms: Sites offering comprehensive data on their own networks, such as engagement, reach, and follower growth, include Facebook Insights, Instagram Insights, and Twitter Analytics.

2. Third-party analytics tools: A variety of third-party applications, like Sprout Social, Hootsuite, and Buffer, provide thorough social media analytics on a number of different platforms.

3. Google **Analytics:** This free tool can provide insights into website traffic and conversions from social media, allowing you to track the impact of your social media efforts on your website.

Tips for Effective Analysis and Actionable Insights

1**. Establish clear objectives**: It's important to have objectives in mind before you analyze your social media data. This will assist you in concentrating on the pertinent metrics and helping you make data-driven choices to enhance your approach.

2. **Evaluate performance over time**: You can spot patterns and trends by monitoring your social media performance over time. This can help you identify what functions well and what

doesn't so you can make the required changes.

3. **Keep an eye on your rivals:** Analyzing your rivals' social media activity can reveal tactics to you and point out areas where you can strengthen your position.

4. **Use data to guide your strategy**: Your upcoming social media marketing initiatives should be guided by the information gathered from social media analytics. Utilize the knowledge acquired to develop campaigns that are more focused and successful.

To sum up, the success of your social media marketing strategy depends on tracking and evaluating your social media performance. You may obtain insightful information and consistently enhance your social media presence by monitoring important indicators and employing the appropriate tools and strategies.

CHAPTER XIV

STAYING UP-TO-DATE WITH SOCIAL MEDIA TRENDS AND CHANGES

Staying current with social media trends and changes is critical for businesses and individuals looking to maintain a competitive advantage in the ever-changing field of digital marketing. By continually monitoring and responding to the newest advancements in social media platforms, algorithms, and user behaviours, businesses may effectively improve their strategy for reaching and engaging with their target audience. Keeping up with developing trends and changes allows for more proactive decision-making, promotes innovation, and improves the overall effectiveness of social media marketing activities. In today's fast-paced digital economy, staying on top of social media trends is critical for long-term success and relevance in the online sphere.

A. The Importance of Staying Current.

The social media landscape is constantly evolving, with new features, trends, and algorithms emerging on a regular basis. To effectively connect and engage with their target audience, small businesses must keep up with these changes. Businesses may stay ahead of the competition and alter their marketing methods to be effective and relevant by staying current with social media trends and advancements.

Ways to Stay Informed

1. Following Influencers and Experts on Social Media

Following industry leaders and influencers is one of the best methods to remain up to date with social media trends. These people frequently see new trends and developments early and are quick to share them with others, offering insightful commentary and pointers on how to apply them to your marketing plan.

2. Taking Part in Virtual Communities

Professionals can exchange experiences, tactics, and insights in a multitude of social media marketing-focused online communities and forums. Businesses can participate in discussions and get knowledge from other members of the industry while staying up to date on the newest trends and changes by joining these communities.

3. Participating in Workshops and Conferences

One of the best ways to keep up with the newest developments in social media marketing is to attend conferences and workshops. These gatherings frequently include thought leaders and professionals in the field who impart their expertise on the latest developments in the social media space.

4. Making Use of Tools for Social Media Analytics

Businesses can gain important information and insights about their audience, content performance, and trends by utilizing social media analytics tools. Businesses can spot any shifts in their audience's behavior and modify their approach by routinely observing these metrics.

Modifications to Marketing Strategy

It is crucial for businesses to integrate any new social media trends or changes into their marketing plans. This could entail exploiting new social media platform capabilities, modifying posting schedules, or developing new content formats. Businesses may maintain their relevance and audience engagement by embracing these changes and remaining flexible.

CONCLUSION

To effectively sell themselves on social media, small businesses must stay abreast of trends and developments in the platform. Through engaging with online communities, attending events, following experts and influencers, and employing analytics tools, organizations may remain up to date and modify their tactics to remain competitive. Maintaining a strong online presence for their brand and keeping up with the always evolving social media landscape require constant strategy monitoring and adjustment.

A. Recap Of Key Points

1. Identify your target audience: The first step in any social media marketing strategy is to identify your target audience. It assists you in modifying your message and content to appeal to the appropriate audience.
2. Select the appropriate platforms: Not every business can benefit from the use of every social media site. Determine which social media channels are most used by your target market and concentrate your efforts there.
3. Create a consistent brand image: The identity and values of your brand should be reflected in your social media profiles. To

increase brand identification, stick to a consistent color scheme, tone, and messaging.
4. Provide interesting content: The main goals of social media are to interact and establish a connection with your audience. To keep your material engaging and new, combine text, photos, videos, and other media.
5. Be consistent and active: Consistency is key in social media marketing. Post regularly and engage with your audience to keep them interested and build a loyal following.
6. Use hashtags: Hashtags help increase your reach and visibility on social media. Use relevant and trending hashtags to reach a wider audience and join relevant conversations.
7. Make use of user-generated content: Posts written by users and customer reviews, for example, can be extremely effective marketing tools. To create social proof, invite your fans to share their interactions with your brand.
8. Interact with your audience: Social media provides a two-way avenue for communication. React to reviews, mails, and comments to demonstrate to your

audience that you respect their thoughts and criticism.
9. Make use of paid advertising: Although organic social media reach is dwindling, paid advertising can assist you in reaching a wider audience and focusing on particular demographics.
10. Analyze and make adjustments: Keep an eye on your social media statistics to see what is and is not effective. To enhance your outcomes, modify your approach correspondingly.

B. Recommendations
1. Define your target audience
2. Choose the right platforms
3. Consistency is key
4. Use high-quality visuals
5. Engage with your audience
6. Utilize hashtags
7. Collaborate with influencers
8. Monitor and analyze your performance
9. Run targeted ads
10. Be authentic and genuine

C. Looking ahead: The Future Of Social Media Marketing For Small Businesses

Social media marketing for small businesses is probably going to keep changing in the future and become even more crucial to their success. Businesses of all sizes are realizing how important it is to have a strong online presence and use social media to engage with their target audience as a result of the growth of social media platforms and the rising use of technology.

The following are some possible patterns and advancements that could influence how small businesses use social media marketing in the future:

1. **A stronger focus on genuine and customized content**
   Businesses will need to figure out how to stand out and establish a more personal connection with their audience as social media becomes more crowded with material. Instead of writing generic or sales-focused blogs, they should create content that is specific to the requirements and interests of their target audience.

2. **The relevance of influencer marketing is rising**
   Influencer marketing is partnering with someone who can effectively reach a large audience on social media and endorse a product or brand. This kind of marketing has shown to be successful in expanding its reach and establishing reputation, thus small firms will probably continue to see an increase in its use.

3. **The steady increase in video material**
   On social media has grown in popularity, and this trend is probably here to stay. To stay current and keep their audience interested, small businesses must use video into their social media strategy.

4. **Using electronic commerce**
   Social media companies are beginning to incorporate shopping elements into their networks as they realize the potential of e-commerce. Small businesses will be able to sell directly to their followers as a result, increasing the significance of social media as a sales-boosting tool.

5. **Application of chatbots and artificial intelligence (AI)**
   Because AI and chatbots may help businesses automate certain processes and enhance customer care, they are becoming more common in social media marketing. To improve user experience and expedite processes, small businesses can begin integrating these tools into their social media operations.

   In summary, the future of social media

marketing for small businesses is probably going to include a focus on authenticity and personalization, influencer marketing, the growth of video content, e-commerce integration, and the usage of chatbots and artificial intelligence. Small businesses may utilize social media to effectively reach and engage their target audience if they keep up with current developments and incorporate them into their plan.

Action Points

1. *Set up profiles on relevant social media platforms:* Start by creating profiles on the most popular and relevant social media platforms for your business, such as Facebook, Twitter, Instagram, and LinkedIn.

2. *Optimize your profiles:* Make sure your profiles are complete with all necessary information, including a profile picture, cover photo, and a short bio that accurately describes your business.

3. *Create a social media content calendar:* Plan out your social media content in advance to ensure consistency and avoid last-minute scrambling. This will also help you maintain a good mix of content types, such as promotional posts, informative posts, and engaging posts.

4. *Use high-quality visuals:* Visual content is more engaging and shareable than text-only posts. Use high-quality images,

videos, and graphics in your social media posts to catch the attention of your audience.

5. Engage with your audience: Social media is a two-way street. Make sure to respond to comments, messages, and mentions from your followers. This will help build a stronger relationship with your audience and improve your brand's reputation.

6. Utilize hashtags: Hashtags can help expand the reach of your posts and make them more discoverable. Do some research to find relevant and popular hashtags in your industry, and use them in your posts.

7. Post consistently: Consistency is key in social media marketing. Make sure to post regularly, ideally at least once a day, to keep your audience engaged and interested in your content.

8. Monitor and track your performance: Use social media analytics tools to track your

performance and see what type of content resonates best with your audience. This will help you adjust your strategy and improve your results.

9. *Run promotions and campaigns: Social media is a great platform for running promotions, contests, and campaigns to engage your audience and attract new followers. Make sure to follow the platform's guidelines and rules when doing so.*

10. *Collaborate with influencers: Partnering with influencers in your industry can help you reach a larger and more targeted audience. Identify influencers who align with your brand and collaborate with them on sponsored posts or campaigns.*

11. *Utilize paid advertising: Social media platforms offer various advertising options to help you reach a wider audience and promote your products or services. Consider setting aside a budget*

for paid advertising to boost your social media presence.

12. *Stay up-to-date on social media trends: Social media is constantly evolving, so it's important to stay informed about new features, algorithm changes, and trends. This will help you stay ahead of the game and make the most out of your social media marketing effort.*

REFERENCES

1. 'The Ultimate Guide to Social Media Marketing for Small Businesses' by Neil Patel - This comprehensive guide covers everything from setting goals to creating a social media strategy, with a focus on small businesses and startups.
2. 'Social Media Marketing for Small Business: A Beginner's Guide' by HubSpot - This beginner-friendly guide covers the basics of social media marketing for small businesses, including tips and best practices.
3. 'Social Media Marketing: The Ultimate Guide for Small Businesses' by Sprout Social - This guide covers the fundamentals of social media marketing, as well as advanced strategies and case studies specifically geared towards small businesses.

4. 'The Young Entrepreneur's Guide to Social Media Marketing' by Peter Voogd - This book offers a unique perspective on social media marketing for small businesses,

with insights from successful young entrepreneurs.

5. 'Social Media Marketing for Small Business: A Step-by-Step Guide to Success' by Ramon Ray - This practical guide provides step-by-step instructions for creating a social media marketing plan and leveraging different platforms to grow your small business.

6. 'The Complete Guide to Social Media for Small Businesses' by Constant Contact - This guide offers tips and advice on how small businesses can effectively use social media to build relationships with customers and drive sales.

7. 'Social Media Marketing for Small Businesses: A Comprehensive Guide' by Hootsuite - This guide covers all aspects of social media marketing for small businesses, including content creation, paid advertising, and analytics.

8. 'The Entrepreneur's Guide to Social Media Marketing' by Susan Gunelius - This book provides a comprehensive overview of social media marketing for entrepreneurs, with practical tips and case studies.

9. 'Social Media Marketing for Small Business: The Power of Local' by DavFe Delaney - This guide focuses on leveraging social media for local small businesses, with tips on how to engage with and attract customers in your community.

10. 'The Small Business Guide to Social Media Marketing' by Gary Vaynerchuk - This book offers a no-nonsense approach to social media marketing for small businesses, with actionable advice and real-world examples.

#smallbusinessmarketing #Facebookforbusiness'

www.ingramcontent.com/pod-product-compliance
Lightning Source LLC
Chambersburg PA
CBHW050113230526
45470CB00004B/1812